Words of Life from the Cross

DAILY DEVOTIONS

MARK W. LOVE

CONCORDIA PUBLISHING HOUSE • SAINT LOUIS

Library of Congress Cataloging-in-Publication Data

Love, Mark W.

Words of Life from the Cross : daily devotions / Mark W. Love.

      p. cm.

ISBN 978-0-7586-1869-6

1. Lent—Prayers and devotions. 2. Lutheran Church–Missouri Synod–Prayers and devotions. I. Title.

BV85.L68 2009

242'.34–cd22

                              2009035705

1 2 3 4 5 6 7 8 9 10   18 17 16 15 14 13 12 11 10 09

INTRODUCTION

The approach in this Lenten series is based on two revelations of God in the following texts:

> But what comes out of the mouth proceeds from the heart, and this defiles a person. For out of the heart come evil thoughts, murder, adultery, sexual immorality, theft, false witness, slander. (Matthew 15:18–19)

> For if anyone thinks he is something, when he is nothing, he deceives himself. (Galatians 6:3)

We often speak of the sinful nature as the "rebel" or our "death within." The sinful nature's orientation is manifested in what are called the seven capital sins of pride, greed, envy, anger, lust, gluttony, and sloth. These are called "capital" because all sins, be they sins of commission or omission, flow out from these seven sins of the heart.

Pride's work in the sinful nature is to insulate the sinner from the reality of his condition, his responsibility to God and his neighbor. Pride does this by casting illusions about our reality, just as Satan did to Adam and Eve. Sinful pride works to keep each of us firm in the belief that we are God—or that we are at least like God.

The seven last words of Christ, spoken on the cross, are seven words of reality spoken by the Son of God, who passively suffers our fallen reality. In this Lenten season, I would have you consider some of the illusions that our sinful pride has cast for all of us, and how the words of Christ crucified embrace and overcome our illusions with the reality of His presence, His passion, His death, and His resurrection.

May the Lord Jesus Christ, who has embraced our reality and given us His through Baptism, humble us and keep us before the saving reality of His Word, His cross, and His resurrection. Amen.

ASH
WEDNESDAY
& THE DAYS
FOLLOWING

The Pardoning Word

Ash Wednesday

When a stepfather tries to set down some rules, his children may declare: "You are not my father." In a similar way, our sinful pride casts the illusion that God is not really our Father, so we do not have to obey Him. God speaks to such illusions: "You turn things upside down! Shall the potter be regarded as the clay, that the thing made should say of its maker, 'He did not make me' " (Isaiah 29:16).

> ## "Father, forgive them, for they know not what they do" (Luke 23:34).

On the cross, Jesus speaks a word that names the relationship of all flesh with God. When Jesus prays "Father," He prays as the Son of Man in the place of man, the place of the broken relationship with God and the place of the cursed.

Naming and claiming our relationship on the cross, Jesus claims our broken relationship with the Father that He might receive the consequences of our break with God as our Father.

Yet even as Jesus prayed as the Son of Man, He also prayed as the Son of God. With the word *Father* prayed on the cross, Jesus speaks and thus creates a new relationship for all human flesh with God as our Father in Him. Christ's resurrection reveals the reality of a new relationship through faith that cannot be broken by sin. "God sent forth His Son . . . to redeem those who were under the law, so that we might receive adoption as sons. . . . God has sent the Spirit of His Son into our hearts, crying, 'Abba! Father!' " (Galatians 4:4–6).

Prayer "O Lord, You are our Father; we are the clay, and You are our potter; we are all the work of Your hand . . . remember not iniquity forever. Behold, please look, we are all Your people." **Isaiah 64:8–9**

The Pardoning Word

Thursday after Ash Wednesday

After Adam and Eve had been deceived by the devil and fallen into sin, the Lord asked Adam, "Have you eaten of the tree of which I commanded you not to eat?" (Genesis 3:11). Adam's response reveals work of sinful pride to deceive him with the illusion that he had no guilt. He said, "The woman whom You gave to be with me, she gave me fruit of the tree, and I ate" (Genesis 3:12). While our sinful pride allows us to acknowledge our wrong, we deny our guilt or responsibility for such wrongs.

> "Father, forgive them, for they know not what they do" (Luke 23:34).

With this petition, Jesus has allowed Himself to be placed in our place by those gleeful to be rid of the reality of God He brings. When Jesus petitions the Father to forgive us, He speaks the reality of our guilt and the justice we are due. Yet in asking that we be forgiven, Jesus is asking far more than we hear. Jesus is saying, "Father, whatever is against them, whatever is due them for their rightful guilt, I would have it to be Mine to deal with, that they might go free from it."

Jesus is requesting the Father to deal with the realities of our guilt and its consequences, which are too great for us. When He cries out, "Why have You forsaken Me?" we know that the Father has made our guilt Jesus' guilt to deal with. The resurrection is the Father's declaration that Christ crucified has taken and dealt with our guilt and overcome all its realities.

Through Baptism we are united to Christ crucified and resurrected, and through faith we enjoy new and eternal realities with God in the midst of the temporal realities of our sinful nature.

Prayer "For Your name's sake, O LORD, pardon my guilt, for it is great." **Psalm 25:11**

The Pardoning Word

Friday after Ash Wednesday

The word *idol* comes from the word *image*. The reality of any image, and thus an idol, is that it is never the real thing. Our sinful pride does not want us to know and believe in the real God because it means the dethronement and death of our sinful nature. Satan casts the illusion for us about God to keep us separated from Him and our neighbor. It was illusions that led people to falsely charge and bring Jesus to be crucified and say boldly, "His blood be on us and on our children!" (Matthew 27:25).

> "Father, forgive them, for they know not what they do" (Luke 23:34).

Having allowed Himself to be brought where man's illusions about God would place Him, Jesus speaks the reality of man's ignorance. He petitions the Father to let Him deal with the ignorance of man that put Him on the cross, so that He might deal with the wrath of the real God on all ignorance.

The most that man's natural knowledge of God can reveal to him is the Law that is now imperfectly written on his heart. Speaking this word on the cross, Jesus is, and He speaks, a greater revelation and reality of God's love and desire for mankind in the forgiveness of sins. This word Jesus speaks is the true God "for" us because of the reality of our sinful ignorance of God. It is through faith in this greater revelation, spoken by and revealed in the Word made flesh, that we may know the true God and eternal life.

Prayer "Make me to know Your ways, O LORD. . . . Lead me in Your truth and teach me, for You are the God of my salvation; for You I wait all the day long." **Psalm 25:4–5**

The Pardoning Word

Saturday after Ash Wednesday

Pride casts the illusion that we do not turn to a priest or intercessor with God, lest we turn to the Lord and be saved from our sin. According to this illusion, our need is determined through feelings. If we do not feel right with God, we are guided by this illusion to do those religious things that make us feel spiritually good and right. Feeling good again, we must be right with God again. This illusion allows us to claim the Scriptures as our truth and Jesus as our Savior, but in reality we have made our feelings the authoritative texts and our actions the means of our rightness with God.

> "Father, forgive them, for they know not what they do" (Luke 23:34).

The reality of our need for an intercessor savior is revealed in Christ's location on the cross and this petitioning word He speaks to God the Father. On the cross, Jesus is secured by man into man's situation so that He might intercede for all. Notice that Jesus does not intercede for Himself, but for us, for those who cannot intercede or save themselves.

With this word, Jesus reveals the reality that He has come to intercede with God on behalf of all people. In this way, Jesus makes peace between God and every one of us through His sacrificial death. The Father answers this petitioning word and declares the success of Christ's intercession when He raises Him from the dead. Through faith in Christ as our High Priest, our High Intercessor, we have the peace of God and the assurance that "if anyone does sin, we have an advocate with the Father, Jesus Christ" (1 John 2:1).

Prayer "Be to me a rock of refuge, to which I may continually come; You have given the command to save me, for You are my rock and my fortress." **Psalm 71:3**

LENT
WEEK ONE

The Pardoning Word

First Sunday in Lent

Our sinful pride seeks to preserve and perpetuate the sinful self. Through its illusions, all kinds of love are a matter of investment. Any act of love is done solely for the sake of the selfish gain. Our enemies are already indebted to us; therefore, we owe them nothing. With this illusion we are able to protect ourselves from further loss and at the same time gain the pleasure of paying them back.

> "Father, forgive them, for they know not what they do" (Luke 23:34).

With this word, Jesus shows the reality of God's love for us, for while we were still sinners, still enemies of God, He saved us from the wrath of God, reconciling us to God (Romans 5:8–10).

Jesus shows God's love to all His enemies, those then and us yet today, who still betray Him, deny Him, falsely accuse Him, judge Him, and reject Him. With this word, He asks the Father to let Him pay the debt, our debt as His enemies.

Through this word, Jesus brings the reality of God's love to bear upon us so that we might be other than the sinful enemies of God we were conceived and born to be. Through His suffering the wrath of God and death, Jesus pays the debt of all God's enemies. His resurrection is God's declaration that Jesus' act of love has paid our debt in full. God no longer looks upon us as His enemies. In Baptism, we are united to Jesus Christ and have the blessed assurance that "if anyone is in Christ, he is a new creation. The old has passed away; behold, the new has come. All this is from God, who through Christ reconciled us to Himself" (2 Corinthians 5:17–18).

Prayer "Make Your face shine on Your servant; save me in Your steadfast love!" **Psalm 31:16**

The Pardoning Word

Monday, Lent 1

It was Cain who first voiced the illusion that "I am not my brother's keeper" in an attempt to free himself from any responsibility for the murder of his brother Abel. In truth, Cain was not the first to embrace this illusion. His father, Adam, denied any responsibility as Eve's keeper by his silence at her offering of and eating the forbidden fruit. Our sinful pride uses this illusion to stifle our ideas or attempts to live for the sake of another, thus thwarting our God-given purpose as His earthly means of good to others.

"Father, forgive them, for they know not what they do" (Luke 23:34).

Everything about Christ, from His birth to His burial, is about Him living beyond Himself to keep His brothers and sisters of the flesh. Now passively suffering at the hands of His brothers and sisters, Jesus intercedes and speaks this petitioning word to His Father for our forgiveness. With this word, Jesus petitions the Father to let Him keep our sins, keep the wrath of God, and keep the death we earned. All that would keep us from God the Father and one another, Jesus has come to keep so that we might be kept free from the power of sin and death.

Jesus is the reality of the Lord living beyond Himself in order to keep us. Christ's resurrection assures us that Jesus now keeps all things and that nothing can interfere with His keeping of us. Through faith in Christ we have His keeping, and we are kept forever in Him. "The LORD will keep you from all evil; He will keep your life" (Psalm 121:7).

Prayer "Wondrously show Your steadfast love, O Savior. . . . Keep me as the apple of Your eye; hide me in the shadow of Your wings." **Psalm 17:7–8**

The Pardoning Word

Tuesday, Lent 1

Calling on the name of the Lord acknowledges our need and dependency on Him. Our sinful nature cannot tolerate such exercises in humility. Our sinful nature would rather contend that prayer does not change things. The illusion is cast first that the sole purpose of prayer is for the Lord to change things according to our bidding. When the Lord fails to act as we bid, sinful pride casts the illusion that prayer is useless.

> ### "Father, forgive them, for they know not what they do" (Luke 23:34).

Near the depths of His humiliation on the cross, Jesus exercises Himself in humility for our sake. With this word of prayer, Jesus petitions the Father to change Him so that the Father might answer His prayer to change us from the guilty to the forgiven.

Jesus makes Himself one with us in our guilt as He has already become one with us in our flesh. This word establishes the reality that the Son of God has come to be changed from the innocent to the guilty, be changed from the pure to the impure, be changed from the living to the dead. Christ prays for this change so that we might be changed through Him from the guilty to the forgiven, the impure to the pure, the dead to the living.

The reality of prayer is that it does change things—us and all those who exercise themselves in faith by calling on the name of the Lord.

While prayer is no Means of Grace, no means of forgiveness, it is the first response of faith for those who receive God's grace and forgiveness. "Nevertheless, not as I will, but as You will" (Matthew 26:39).

Prayer "Answer me when I call. . . . You have given me relief when I was in distress. Be gracious to me and hear my prayer!" **Psalm 4:1**

The Promising Word

Wednesday, Lent 1

W e are born with hearts that are bound in sin to an investment kind of love. The sinful nature can only give love when another has earned its love. Thus, any form of friendship is based on this same investment model. With this kind of love and illusion about friendship, people are saved from living beyond themselves.

> "Truly, I say to you, today you will be with Me in Paradise" (Luke 23:43).

Jesus, unjustly condemned on the cross, speaks the reality of friendship in this word to one who was justly condemned. Confined in his condemnation as we all are, there was no way for this man, or us, to earn the word of friendship Jesus speaks to him. With the unearned gifts of friendship and the word of friendship, Jesus gives this man the unearned and undeserved blessing of paradise. All this friendship flows from God's own kind of love that sent His Son to live and die, not for friends but for strangers and enemies. And this Jesus does because He was not ashamed to be the friend of sinners.

This kind of love and friendship is neither logical nor just. It is God's divine grace. Through His befriending of us on the cross, Jesus receives what is just for us, so that we might receive the logical ends of divine love—our unearned salvation. Paradise is now ours through faith in Jesus Christ and His all-befriending word that He speaks to us.

"Greater love has no one than this, that someone lay down his life for his friends" (John 15:13).

Prayer "Remember not the sins of my youth or my transgressions; according to Your steadfast love remember me, for the sake of Your goodness, O LORD!" **Psalm 25:7**

The Promising Word

Thursday, Lent 1

Our sinful nature contends that our past is no one else's business. We would cast this illusion to hide the reality that our past, along with its consequences, is beyond our control. Our sinful nature is bound in sin to the Law. The only way the Law conducts business with our past is by condemning us in the present and the future. So it casts this illusion in an attempt to save us from the Law.

> "Truly, I say to you, today you will be with Me in Paradise" (Luke 23:43).

Sin leaves us at odds with God. There is a debt that is owed, business that is yet to be concluded. Everyone has this past. And the result is a future they cannot deal with. Out of love for His creation, God sent Jesus to conduct our business and pay our debt.

With this word promising paradise to a man who had not earned it, Jesus assures the man that He has made the man's past, present, and future His business. So mightily does Jesus make this man's past, present, and future His business that He offers him a future that is completely severed from his past, his present, and the future he deserves. This blessed word Jesus speaks to this man and all who humbly repent and believe in Him is not the business of the Law, but the business of God's saving grace.

Through daily repentance in faith, we ask the Lord Jesus to make our business His business. The blessed absolution is Jesus' sure word that He has dealt with our business, and paradise is our blessed dividend. "I will not forget you. Behold, I have engraved you on the palms of My hands" (Isaiah 49:15–16).

Prayer "Forgive us our debts . . . deliver us from evil." Amen.
Matthew 6:12–13

The Promising Word

Friday, Lent 1

All suffering is the result of sin as either a direct consequence of our actions or an indirect consequence of the sinfulness of fallen mankind. Our sinful nature makes its appeals through the illusion that we do not ever deserve to suffer, because to acknowledge that we do would be self-condemning. Such deceiving appeals are made in the hopes that we might rise up and judge God, the righteous Judge, and condemn Him.

> "Truly, I say to you, today you will be with Me in Paradise" (Luke 23:43).

Affixed to the cross, Jesus has come to receive and deal with the reality of divine justice and suffering we all rightly deserve for sin. This word of promised paradise was given to a man who, in faith, confessed the reality of both his guilt and his suffering Christ crucified. Knowing that his suffering is just, he appeals to Christ for something greater than the justice he deserves. This word of promised paradise is Jesus' response to the man and to all who humbly repent and believe in Him.

Fulfilling the demands of justice and suffering, Jesus here speaks a word of divine grace that freely does for us what we cannot do to make ourselves right with God and His courts of divine justice. The resurrection of Christ is God's testimony that Jesus is this greater word, and He has met and overcome all earthly and divine justice for all people.

This greater word of grace is freely spoken to all. This word, like Jesus Christ, does not bring an end to earthly suffering. It does, however, empty all our suffering of its verdict against us and fills it with Jesus Christ for us now and in paradise.

Prayer "Let Your steadfast love comfort me according to Your promise to Your servant." **Psalm 119:76**

The Promising Word

Saturday, Lent 1

Sinful pride's illusion is that Jesus is not my king. The purpose of this illusion would seem to set ourselves up as kings. Yet, in truth, our sinful pride casts this illusion in an attempt to prevent what the Jews feared would happen to them after Jesus had raised Lazarus from the tomb—lose their place (John 11:48).

> "Truly, I say to you, today you will be with Me in Paradise" (Luke 23:43).

This ruling word is spoken to a man who, by his sin, had lost his place in this world and in heaven. Suspended between earth and heaven, the man petitioned Jesus to be his King and rule over him so that he might have a place in His kingdom.

So Jesus, forfeiting His place in heaven and earth, reigns from the throne of Calvary. Ruling over the dominion of the lost given to Him, Jesus speaks this reigning word, and the man has a place in His kingdom. Jesus speaks this reigning word, and the reality of His dominion makes a place for us in paradise.

In Baptism, Jesus speaks a reigning word, and we are given a place in Him and in His kingdom. In Christ, we live in His kingdom and await His coming to take us to the place He has prepared for all those who believe in this King of kings.

Prayer "Give attention to the sound of my cry, my King and my God, for to You do I pray." **Psalm 5:2**

LENT
WEEK TWO

The Promising Word

Second Sunday in Lent

The word *absolve* comes from the Latin *absolvere*, which is "to loosen." To believe in the illusion that we do not need absolution is to believe one of two very false things: First, we are not bound, and therefore do not need to be loosened or absolved by anyone. Second, if we are bound, we can loosen ourselves without anyone's help. Through this illusion, we are deceived that the reality of bondage and only divine help can bring true humility and freedom.

> "Truly, I say to you, today you will be with Me in Paradise" (Luke 23:43).

Inasmuch as all people are bound in the reality of sin and death, Jesus allows Himself to be bound, so that He might speak this loosening, absolving word to the bound. Jesus speaks this loosing word to a man who openly confessed his bondage and the justness of it. Knowing the reality of his just bondage, he also knew the reality of his helplessness in his bondage. Humbled under these realities, all far too great for him, the man cries out to Christ to remember him in His kingdom.

Jesus comes as God's greater reality to face and suffer the realities of our bondage to sin, death, and the wrath of God. Even in the midst of His last hours on the cross, this man lived those hours by a new reality that Jesus' word created and gave to him. Yes, this man would suffer the agony of crucifixion for his crime; neither his suffering nor his death could destroy the fact that he was now loosened, now absolved, to be paradise bound in Christ.

Such is the reality of all who humbly repent and believe on the Lord Jesus Christ.

Prayer "Let my plea come before You; deliver me according to Your word." **Psalm 119:170**

The Promising Word

Monday, Lent 2

Rarely will our sinful nature allow anyone to openly believe he or she is a counselor of God. Yet faith in this illusion is heard in the confessions telling God and others how He ought to be and what He ought to do as God. Living this illusion is heard in the condemning verdicts on the Lord's reasons, means, timings, and locations for accomplishing His will.

> "Truly, I say to you, today you will be
> with Me in Paradise" (Luke 23:43).

Throughout His earthly ministry, Jesus was inundated with those who thought they were His counselors. From age 12 with His parents, in the temple, to the Jewish leaders, to His own disciples, all tried to tell Him how He ought to be and what He ought to do as their Messiah. As the Son of God, Jesus has come as God's Counsel—the Word made flesh to suffer the illusions of sinful human counsel. By that counsel, He is brought to the place where sinful human counsel always brings a person—the place of condemnation and death.

In this place of human counsel, Jesus the Wonderful Counselor speaks this word to will and work the divine counsel that this man and all men should be saved. With this word, Jesus saves that which God would have saved—humanity. With this word, Jesus saves us all, not according to the reasons, the means, the timing, the location of human counsel, but all according to God's own kind of love in Christ.

According to the Counsel of God, Jesus makes it clear with this word from the cross that paradise is the free gift to all who humbly repent and believe in God's Counsel—Jesus Christ.

Prayer "You guide me with Your counsel, and afterward You will receive me to glory." **Psalm 73:24**

The Promising Word

Tuesday, Lent 2

Nothing can be lonelier than suffering. Our sinful nature would always have us lonely or alone. In our sinful pride we contend that inasmuch as we cannot fully voice our pain and suffering, God must be equally limited in His ability to help us in the midst of it. Through this illusion, we are tempted to turn to other would-be helpers who are at best a distraction from our suffering and its real cause.

> "Truly, I say to you, today you will be with Me in Paradise" (Luke 23:43).

God's help, Jesus Christ, speaks this helping, this healing, this comforting word to a man alone in the place of those who deserve no help, no healing, no comfort, no companion. Jesus is God's help for us in all our suffering because He came to stand and suffer in the place of all those alienated from God by sin. So on the cross, with no one to help, He received our sin, our death, and all that makes us alone. He saved us from the cause of all our loneliness and suffering. Yes, He came to fill the place of the lonely and the suffering so that in all our suffering, we might have Him who fully knows our suffering and freely fills it and us with His victorious help.

Christ's bodily resurrection reveals that all human suffering has been emptied of its power to make us alone and alienate us from God, His love, and the blessed paradise He's promised in this word. "I will never leave you nor forsake you" (Hebrews 13:5).

Prayer "Be not far from me, for trouble is near, and there is none to help. Make haste to help me, O Lord, my salvation!" **Psalm 22:11; 38:22**

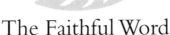

The Faithful Word

Wednesday, Lent 2

Those living by the illusion that there does not have to be consequences for sin usually respond with the rhetorical "What's the big deal?" Helpless in sin, we cannot deal with the just consequences. Our sinful pride would keep this reality from us, lest we humble ourselves and turn to the only one who can deal with our earthly and divine consequences.

In reality, every sin of thought, word, or deed is a rejection of God. It is a declaration that in what we would think, say, or do, we do not want God involved. Inasmuch as God punishes sin by giving us what we want, the consequence for sin is the rejection and absence of God.

> "Eli, Eli, lema sabachthani?" that is, "My God, My God, why have You forsaken Me?" (Matthew 27:46).

With this word, Jesus testifies to the reality of sin and its consequences—the eternal absence of God. Yet by this same word, Jesus testifies to even greater reality—He is suffering the absence of God for us so that we might have fellowship of God.

Jesus speaks this testimony at the "Accounts Payable Counter" called Calvary. By His blood, the check is written, and by the absence of God, the payment is processed. The Easter resurrection is God's testimony that Christ covered the cost and overcame all the consequences of our sin.

As the Holy Spirit unites us to Christ in Baptism, we receive the blessed consequences of our Savior's perfectly lived life, sacrificial death, and victorious resurrection. Through faith, we live daily in the consequences of a Savior who would not and will not ever leave us or forsake us.

Prayer "Save me, O God! For the waters have come up to my neck. I sink in deep mire, where there is no foothold; I have come into deep waters, and the flood sweeps over me." **Psalm 69:1–2**

The Faithful Word

Thursday, Lent 2

In the midst of suffering, we can succumb to the illusion that we go through hell on earth. This illusion erodes any proper understanding of hell, its purpose, and the one who created and assigns people to it. Through this illusion, sinful pride seeks to convince people that a God who let them suffer must have rejected them and is not to be trusted.

> "Eli, Eli, lema sabachthani?" that is, "My God, My God, why have You forsaken Me?" (Matthew 27:46).

With this word of reality, Jesus establishes what hell really is. It is being left physically, emotionally, mentally, and spiritually alone. It is to be without God, who inwardly renews us, though outwardly we are wasting away. It is to be without God, whose mercies are new every morning. It is to be without God, who restores the soul. It is to be without God, whose love is at work in all things for good. It is to be without God, who makes us alive, even though we are dying and dead.

Inasmuch as we in our sin have chosen to think, speak, and act alone and without God, hell is the place that we have chosen; hell is the place from which we cannot set ourselves free. Out of love for us and all mankind, God sends His own Son to this place without God, so that we might be given a better place as children of God.

Having been left alone in the place of those who deserve this eternal aloneness, Jesus speaks this word as our Blessed Savior from hell. With this word, Jesus makes it clear that in Him we are not, and shall never be, left physically, emotionally, mentally, and spiritually alone.

Prayer "Turn to me and be gracious to me, for I am lonely and afflicted." **Psalm 25:16**

The Faithful Word

Friday, Lent 2

Maybe we are suffering, justly or unjustly. Maybe we have been rejected or simply not chosen. Perhaps we are not the best at something. Maybe we did not get or do not have what we think we deserve. The only explanation the sinful pride will allow for such contrary situations is that God has abandoned us. Accordingly, with this illusion, if God were with us, all things would be for us.

> "Eli, Eli, lema sabachthani?" that is, "My God, My God, why have You forsaken Me?" (Matthew 27:46).

Out of a desperate love and want for every person, Jesus allowed Himself to be brought to the place of those who in and by their sin have abandoned God. In the rightful place of sinners, Jesus Christ, the Son of God, is. And here He speaks the reality that God is with us. He came to this place not to abandon us, but to be abandoned, so that through Him we might be brought back to God, our Source of all that is good, gracious, and right. This word assures us that even in our sin we shall find the Son of God there to save and deliver us into the kingdom of His grace.

In Baptism, the Holy Spirit unites us to Jesus Christ through simple water and His Word, and we are new creations. Yet, before that baptismal word of grace could be spoken to us, Jesus had to speak this word of Law from the cross for us. Before this saving baptismal union with Christ could ever be ours, the abandonment of the damned had to be united to Him.

Through faith in Christ and this assuring word, we have peace and the presence of God for us in all things.

Prayer "Rise up; come to our help! Redeem us for the sake of Your steadfast love!" **Psalm 44:26**

The Faithful Word

Saturday, Lent 2

No one can know how alone I am." As with all illusions, this one contains an element of truth. In truth, no other human can fully know our sense and awareness of loneliness. No one can fully know just how alone our sin has made us. This illusion is used by our sinful pride to convince us of our helpless isolation from all others and any potential help. This illusion tends to foster destructive and sometimes deadly behavior in those caught in its deception.

> "Eli, Eli, lema sabachthani?" that is, "My God, My God, why have You forsaken Me?" (Matthew 27:46).

God sent His Son into our human flesh and to journey into our aloneness. It is not the glimpses of aloneness that we suffer in this life, but the total aloneness we have made for ourselves in sin. This word, this cry, tells us that Jesus suffered the divine alienation and loneliness we deserve for our sin.

With this word, Jesus declares that our alienation from God is over as He has reconciled us to God through this suffering. Even in death we shall now find Him there to guide us into the glory He has prepared for all who believe in Him.

In the blessed Sacrament of Holy Communion, we receive the body and blood of Jesus Christ crucified, dead, and buried alone for us. In this blessed Communion, the Lord comes to us to receive what is ours. In that same moment, He gives and fills us with Himself and all that is Him and His.

For those who believe in Him, there are no moments, no tragedies, no suffering, no loneliness that He does not fill with Himself and His victorious resurrection.

Prayer "Hear my prayer, O LORD, and give ear to my cry; hold not Your peace at my tears! For I am a sojourner with You, a guest."
Psalm 39:12

LENT
WEEK THREE

The Faithful Word

Third Sunday in Lent

I n the wake of tragedy, sinful pride will contend that God and His ways cannot be trusted. Unable to grasp or see any good in a tragedy, our sinful nature comes to the only conclusion that God has betrayed us. So this illusion is cast in an attempt to keep us from trusting the Lord.

> "Eli, Eli, lema sabachthani?" that is,
> "My God, My God, why have You
> forsaken Me?" (Matthew 27:46).

With this word, the Son of God asks the "Why?" that sin has put upon the lips and hearts of all those conceived and bound in sin. God chose to have His Son suffer such divine and eternal silence to save us from the eternal silence we have chosen in our sin. He has been made to suffer the silence of God, not for His sin, but for ours. Jesus trusts His Father and His ways enough to remain on the cross, suffering our pain and silence for us. Jesus' trust in God and His ways enable Him to do more than remain alone in divine silence. His trust speaks His last word in death as He commended His spirit into the hands of the God who had forsaken Him.

Our Lord gives and works this faith in all the baptized. As our Savior, Christ does not need to eliminate or explain those times when God's ways lead us through the valley of the shadow of death. What faith in Christ does is fill each of those ways and valleys with Him who is at work in all of this for our good.

Prayer "Rescue me, O my God . . . You, O Lord, are my hope, my trust, O Lord, from my youth." **Psalm 71:4–5**

The Faithful Word

Monday, Lent 3

Only in sheer sinful pride can one contend, "I have never forsaken God." The goal of this illusion is that we be adequately deceived about the reality of sin and thus its consequences. In this way, we will not be deterred in our sin or see any need for the Savior from it.

God punishes sin by giving sinners what they want (Romans 1). Sin is a denial that God alone is the source of all that is truly good, gracious, and right for us. Sin, in whatever form, is the absence of God. So when God punishes sin, He rejects and leaves one alone without God and without anything good, gracious, and right.

> "Eli, Eli, lema sabachthani?" that is, "My God, My God, why have You forsaken Me?" (Matthew 27:46).

By this word, Jesus speaks the reality of what sin is and of its consequence, because having received all our sin, He is now without God or anything that is truly good, gracious, and right. God has given Him what we want in every sin we commit.

Having spoken this word, Jesus remains in the reality of our sin and its consequence so we might know that He will never leave us nor forsake us. His resurrection assures us that Jesus has met the reality of our sin and overcome it with the reality of God's love.

Through faith in Christ, we receive the want and desire of God's heart—our salvation from the realities of sin, death, and hell.

Prayer "Though I walk through the valley of the shadow of death, I will fear no evil, for You are with me." **Psalm 23:4**

The Faithful Word

Tuesday, Lent 3

God asks through the prophet Malachi, "A son honors his father. . . . If then I am a father, where is My honor?" (1:6). To honor is to give preference to another over self. Our sinful pride honors self above all else. Sinful pride casts the illusion that our relationship with God is not broken and we should give preference to ourselves above all else. If we were to know the brokenness of our relationship with God, we might seek a Great Physician to heal and make us one with God, and this our sinful pride cannot allow.

> "Eli, Eli, lema sabachthani?" that is, "My God, My God, why have You forsaken Me?" (Matthew 27:46).

Jesus speaks this word in the midst of suffering for our sin. This word speaks the reality that sin is a break in every relationship we have. Notice that in this word, Jesus says "My God" and not "My Father." Each sin is our rejection of and a break from God as our Father. The consequences for such sin is that God will forever reject and break from us as our Father and God, as our source of all that is good, gracious, and right for us.

Loving us and wanting a new relationship with us, God gave Jesus to suffer the Father's break from us that we deserve. Jesus honored God as His Father and ours, receiving our sin, our brokenness from God and His break from us, so that we might receive a whole new relationship with God as our Father through Christ.

Through faith in Jesus Christ, we become children of God, "who were born, not of blood nor of the will of the flesh nor of the will of man, but of God" (John 1:13).

Prayer Our Father who art in heaven, Thine is the glory forever and ever. Amen.

The Compassionate Word

Wednesday, Lent 3

Eve's first sin was a rejection of her relationship with God as He created it. Her second sin was a rejection of her relationship with Adam as God had created it. Adam, in his refusal to keep Eve from eating the forbidden fruit, also rejected both His relationship with God and with Eve. To believe that we have no obligation to our neighbor is to serve one's self and nothing else and then to seek to justify our sins of omission.

> "Woman, behold, your son!" . . .
> "Behold, your mother!" (John 19:26–27).

Jesus hung on the cross because He lived His love for all His flesh-bound neighbors. Looking not to His own welfare but to the welfare of His mother, Jesus speaks this word of love to John that he might love Mary as his mother. Notice that Jesus is in the midst of His suffering without any love of a neighbor to help Him in His need. At this time He speaks this loving word to Mary for her welfare in the midst of her suffering. With this word, Jesus does more than give John to His mother and His mother to John. With this word, Jesus gives all of us back to one another in Him so that we might be there for the welfare of one another.

Jesus loves us as Himself so that through His death and resurrection He might make us fellow heirs with Him in heaven. As the Holy Spirit unites us to Christ that we might be given back to God, this baptismal union gives us back to one another in Christ. Through faith in Christ, we have a communion with the saints. And in this communion, we love one another because He first loved us.

Prayer "Let Your steadfast love, O Lord, be upon us, even as we hope in You." **Psalm 33:22**

The Compassionate Word

Thursday, Lent 3

Sinful pride emboldens children to live as if they are free from any accountability to parents. This sinful illusion emboldens them to live as if they are free from any responsibility for their parents. Inasmuch as being inconvenienced by another person has become almost the equivalent to being mugged, this illusion has gained a considerable following. In essence, this illusion seeks to obscure the word *honor* in the Fourth Commandment.

> "Woman, behold, your son!" . . .
> "Behold, your mother!" (John 19:26–27).

Everything about Jesus Christ involves the word *honor* in the Fourth Commandment. To honor someone is to "give preference to" that person in deference to self. From His conception to the grave, everything about Jesus is to honor His heavenly Father.

On the cross, Jesus suffers and dies because of our irresponsibility toward our parents. With this word from the cross, Jesus lives the reality of our responsibility to and for our parents. Notice how in the midst of honoring His Father God by suffering for the salvation of the world, Jesus rightly honors His Father God by also honoring His earthly mother. Jesus does not let His suffering for the sins of every man, woman, and child keep Him from providing for the earthly needs of His mother. In Christ there is forgiveness and reconciliation in our heavenly and earthly families.

In Baptism, we are born into a new relationship with God the Father and our parents. Through faith in Christ, our responsibility to them is no longer born of obligation but born of the sacrificial love that took responsibility for us and our welfare.

Prayer "Let Your work be shown to Your servants, and Your glorious power to their children. Let the favor of the Lord our God be upon us, and establish the work of our hands upon us; yes, establish the work of our hands!" **Psalm 90:16–17**

The Compassionate Word

Friday, Lent 3

The pain and suffering at the loss of a loved one is so great that it often isolates those who grieve. In this sense of isolation, sinful pride casts the illusion that God has no regard for us in our loss. This illusion would have a person believe that the all-knowing Creator and Keeper of life had no regard for the survivors of one He allowed to die. The belief would have such people say, "Surely God knew how much I loved and needed this person; clearly He must have given no thought, no regard to my having to suffer this loss."

> "Woman, behold, your son!" . . .
> "Behold, your mother!" (John 19:26–27).

In reality, Jesus Christ is God's regard for the fallen. Mindful of our lostness and our inability to find our way back to God or one another, God sent His Son to be mindful of our need and of us.

With this word from the cross, Jesus is mindful of His mother's suffering at the loss of her son. So mindful is He that He makes provision for her in her loss. His provision does not give back what she will lose in His impending death, but it does give her what the all-knowing God says will meet her need. One of the hardest things for us to grasp is that God's regard for us is according to our need, not our loss.

With this word, Jesus is and speaks the reality of God's regard, God's thoughtfulness of every human in our loss of things heavenly and earthly. Through faith in Jesus Christ, we receive God's regard and His provision for us according to our need in the midst of our loss.

Prayer "O God my Lord, deal on my behalf for Your name's sake. . . . For I am poor and needy." **Psalm 109:21–22**

The Compassionate Word

People of faith often struggle to understand events that seem to deny God's love and protection. Because they cannot grasp how God could allow or work any good through such events, sinful pride casts the illusion that God can only handle so many things. Many trust in this illusion because it seems to ease the tension such events create. The goal of such an illusion is not the saving of God for us, but the shifting of our faith to another god who is lesser and limited, to a god who is not the true God.

> "Woman, behold, your son!" . . .
> "Behold, your mother!" (John 19:26–27).

There was no greater evil in all of human history than the crucifixion of the innocent Son of God and Son of Mary. He suffers this evil not to stop it or put an end to evil but to receive it and the sin that causes it.

On the cross Jesus suffers the evil of perverted justice. He deals with all the evil that is in the heart of every person throughout time and the evil of every sin that has been or ever will be committed. He prepares to deal with the wrath of God against all this evil. In the midst of handling all this, Jesus speaks this word of reality that He is at work in all things for good. He does not let go of His mother and her need but rather addresses it and meets her need and the needs of all mankind.

Our faith in Christ does not mean that we can handle or even comprehend all the things that happen to us. Through the gift of faith, we receive the one in whom all things are held together—Jesus Christ.

Prayer "For You, O LORD, have made me glad by Your work; at the works of Your hands I sing for joy." **Psalm 92:4**

LENT
WEEK FOUR

The Compassionate Word

Fourth Sunday in Lent

In our sinful pride we think, God owes me for what I have done. Through pride's illusion, God is made the debtor who either never completely pays what He owes us, or when He does pay, it is never on time. Who would put faith in such a God?

> "Woman, behold, your son!" . . .
> "Behold, your mother!" (John 19:26–27).

If anyone has done something great for the Lord, it could be argued that it was Mary, the mother of Jesus. She alone in all of history is the one through whom the Son of God became incarnate and entered the world. According to the illusion above, it would seem as if the Son of God owes Mary a very great deal. However, with this word from the cross, Jesus speaks the reality that for all Mary had done for Him, she was not and is not owed anything. If Jesus owed her, He would not be leaving her. As a sinner, Mary was blessed, not because of what she did, but because God favored her, worked faith in her, and worked His will through her.

As sinners we are blessed and receive all of God's blessings, not because of what we have done or ever will do, but because of what Christ alone has done for us. Through faith in Christ, our work becomes good, not because we have done it, but rather because He has perfected it along with us. Even when we have done these works, we humbly confess the reality Jesus taught us: "So you also, when you have done all that you were commanded, say, 'We are unworthy servants; we have only done what was our duty' " (Luke 17:9–10).

Prayer "Forgive us our debts." **Matthew 6:12**

The Compassionate Word

Monday, Lent 4

In our sin we pridefully think that if we are faithful enough to God, we will be spared suffering. By this illusion, if a person is suffering, then it would have them believe that it is because they are not faithful enough, and it would turn them back to their own works. Ultimately, it leads the sufferer away from God's gracious offer and into despair.

> "Woman, behold, your son!" . . .
> "Behold, your mother!" (John 19:26–27).

Simeon had promised Mary that she would suffer: "A sword will pierce through your own soul also" (Luke 2:35). Who was more faithful to Jesus in earthly terms than His mother, Mary? She had nursed and raised Him, and now here she stands with her dying Son. Yet all her faithfulness did not stop Jesus from speaking these words that pierced her soul.

For all her faithfulness to Jesus, she was still a sinner whose faithfulness had also fallen short of the glory of God (Romans 3:23). To save her and the rest of the world from our lack of true faithfulness, Jesus could not spare her this piercing painful word by which He severs her from Himself. Even in this word that brings Mary pain, He is faithful to her. With this word, Jesus meets her earthly needs so that He can meet her spiritual need.

Faith does not guarantee that we will never suffer. Faith is given to us that we might receive certain hope in Jesus Christ, for He is God's guarantee that no amount or length of suffering can ever separate us from His ever-faithful love and deliverance through it all.

Prayer "Turn to me and be gracious to me, for I am lonely and afflicted. . . . Consider my affliction and my trouble, and forgive all my sins." **Psalm 25:16, 18**

The Compassionate Word

Tuesday, Lent 4

Inasmuch as it is a mystery as to how a woman conceived and born sinful could conceive and give birth to the sinless Son of God, to think that Mary was without sin is to eliminate that mystery. This illusion creates an even greater illusion: that Mary was conceived and born without sin. This, like all of our sinful pride's illusions, seeks to diminish the dependency on divine and elevate the necessity of human. In this way, our faith is shifted away from God's sole role in our salvation to some illusion of human contribution.

> "Woman, behold, your son!" . . .
> "Behold, your mother!" (John 19:26–27).

When Jesus speaks this word to Mary, He does not title her "mother" according to her vocation. By titling Mary "woman," Jesus speaks the reality of her common bondage to sin with all mankind. With this word, Jesus establishes the same relationship with Mary as He had with the thief on the cross. For if Mary was to be saved, then she would have to look to her Son not for the honor due her as His mother but for His undeserved gift of love and forgiveness.

Jesus knew that Mary needed to be saved like the rest of humanity, so He discharges her from her vocation as mother so that she might begin her vocation as the redeemed child of God. With this word Jesus set Mary free from her vocation so that she could receive His blessing of His vocation. As the Lord unites us with Himself in Baptism, He frees us from our vocations so that we might receive the heavenly blessings of His vocation—life and salvation.

Prayer "Behold, I was brought forth in iniquity, and in sin did my mother conceive me. Purge me with hyssop, and I shall be clean; wash me, and I shall be whiter than snow." **Psalm 51:5, 7**

The Suffering Word

Wednesday, Lent 4

Our sinful nature is limited in its understanding of God to what is referred to as "natural" knowledge. This knowledge is limited to God's powerful and majestic work of creation, His works through the realms of nature and human history, and the Law of God written on each person's heart. Because we are bound by sin to this limited understanding of God, He is too powerful, too great, and too righteous for us to come to Him or call upon Him. In response to this, sinful pride proposes that God is not approachable and seeks to keep the sinner from hearing the better word of the Gospel that reveals God as merciful, gracious, and receiving of all.

"I thirst" (John 19:28).

Even while Jesus hangs physically weak on the cross, He is the Son of God who has all authority in heaven and on earth. With such position and power, Jesus could call legions of angels to bring Him the purest of water to refresh Him, yet He does not. Instead, with this word, Jesus speaks the reality that there is no limitation on how lowly and humble God will be to meet and receive those lowly and humbled in their sin.

With this word, Jesus meets us in our sinful limitations, so that He might approach God and His Law for us and suffer its unlimited consequences against our sin.

Jesus Christ is God's better word by which we receive a "revealed" knowledge. In His thirst and His death, Jesus meets us. In His resurrection, He opens the way to God for us so that we may through faith "receive mercy and find grace to help in time of need" (Hebrews 4:16).

Prayer "You, O Lord, are a God merciful and gracious, slow to anger and abounding in steadfast love and faithfulness. Turn to me and be gracious to me." **Psalm 86:15–16**

The Suffering Word

Thursday, Lent 4

Weakness brings the reality that a person is not, and often is unable to be, as others are or they themselves would like to be. Weakness, therefore, in whatever form it may be endured, is often extremely humbling. Our sinful nature will not tolerate such humiliation. In our sinful pride, we try to cover our weakness with the illusion that God does not understand what it is to be weak. This illusion isolates God from us, lest we turn to Him and find Him there with us.

"I thirst" (John 19:28).

All human weakness is a consequence of sin. With this word, Jesus is the reality of God in the midst of all human sin bound in weakness. Jesus allows Himself to become weak and to suffer so that He might save us from the cause of all our weakness—sin.

Like all weakness, Jesus' weakness is a consequence though not of sin, but of love for us even in the midst of our deserved weakness. Jesus allows Himself to become weak to meet us all in our sin-born and sin-bound weakness. With this word, the Son of God takes our weakness to Himself so that He might take it with Him into death.

This word of Christ is the reality that God is with us in our weakness. Christ's death is the reality that God is with us in our greatest weakness. And Christ's resurrection tells the entire world that He is our victorious strength in all our weakness.

Prayer "Incline Your ear to me; rescue me speedily! Be a rock of refuge for me, a strong fortress to save me!" **Psalm 31:2**

The Suffering Word

Friday, Lent 4

With a heart inscribed with the Law, we know that we must do something for the poor and the needy. The Law also accuses us of not caring or doing enough. Committed to protecting us from these realities of the Law, our sinful pride tells us that God does not care about the poor and needy, shifting the blame from us and onto God. By affixing the blame for the poverty and need of others on God, our sinful pride also seeks to set us free from assuming any responsibility for helping others.

"I thirst" (John 19:28).

With this word, the Son of God became the poor and the needy. With His cry, "My God, My God, why have You forsaken Me?" (Matthew 27:46), the Son of God became the reality of the poor and needy of soul.

The reality of God's love and care for the poor and needy is found in His sending His Son to give up all that is His to become the poor and needy. This, our Lord says, is "the grace of our Lord Jesus Christ, that though He was rich, yet for your sake He became poor, so that you by His poverty might become rich" (2 Corinthians 8:9).

Having received Christ's poverty on the cross and the riches of His resurrection in Baptism, we live a new life by faith. Through this new life, God reaches out to care for and meet the needs of those around us. In this way, we live as He created us to be: living, breathing distribution centers of His good according to the needs around us.

Prayer "O God my Lord . . . because Your steadfast love is good, deliver me! For I am poor and needy, and my heart is stricken within me." **Psalm 109:21–22**

The Suffering Word

Saturday, Lent 4

Our sinful pride whispers, "I put God and others before myself." This illusion is cast so that we might believe that we have kept the whole Law of God, that we love God and love our neighbor as ourselves. Sinful pride seeks to paint this Law in shades of gray in an attempt to protect us from the reality of our bondage in sin.

"I thirst" (John 19:28).

As our God-sent Savior, Jesus was sent to do for us what we cannot do to be right with God. His doing, and His way of doing all things, is our doing of them through faith in Him. If considered in isolation, Jesus, speaking this word for His own refreshment, might appear as if He put Himself before God and others. The timing of this word for Himself reveals the reality of our need for Him to put God and others before Himself. This word of Christ comes only after He has put God the Father and others before Himself.

Before Jesus spoke this word for self, He spoke a word for the forgiveness of all others. He spoke a word to provide for His mother, and then He spoke a word providing for God's need to punish for the sins of all others. Only after He has loved His Father with all His heart, soul, strength, and mind, and loving us as Himself, did Jesus speak a word for Himself.

Through faith in Christ, we receive His sequence and timetable of love for God and our neighbor. In that faith, we live to put God before all things so that we might put others before ourselves and thus fulfill the law of Christian love.

Prayer "Wash me thoroughly from my iniquity, and cleanse me from my sin! For I know my transgressions, and my sin is ever before me." **Psalm 51:2–3**

LENT
WEEK FIVE

The Suffering Word

Fifth Sunday in Lent

When one has to do without, sinful pride looks past the reason and focuses on simply being alone. Accordingly, one is convinced that no one else, not even God, can know what it is like to do without.

In this illusion, God's Word is deemed useless because it is ignorant of one's situation. Prayer becomes equally useless because God cannot help what He does not know about.

"I thirst" (John 19:28).

With this word, Jesus testifies that He is in the place our sin has brought us, the place of those who deserve to be without all things in heaven and earth. Now without His heavenly Father, who has forsaken Him in our sin, Jesus calls out in His physical agony for some earthly refreshment as He approaches death. With the offer of vinegar made to Him, Jesus experiences the reality that there is nothing earthly to comfort or refresh Him, or anyone else, in death.

Oh, glory of this word, for He who was the rock from which flowed water for His people in the desert chose to suffer without any water. He who turned water into wine chose to do without water or wine. He speaks this word and does without because by our sin we are without. Jesus knows and became the reality of our "withoutness," so that in Him, we might receive all things.

Today we enjoy living water that Jesus offers to one and all in the dry and sinful land of without. We first sip of this living water at the baptismal font. We live by faith beside this water so that in all things, we, and our souls, are refreshed even in death to eternal life.

Prayer "O God, You are my God; earnestly I seek You; my soul thirsts for You . . . as in a dry and weary land where there is no water." **Psalm 63:1**

The Suffering Word

Monday, Lent 5

When, despite all efforts, we suffer, we are forced to confront the reality that we are not God. Our sinful pride seeks to save us from such realities and thus casts the illusion that God's will is not always the best thing.

Through this illusion, our sinful pride would ultimately bring us to the belief that neither God nor His Word should then be trusted.

"I thirst" (John 19:28).

In all that Jesus has suffered to this point in His crucifixion, He chose to allow it to happen to Him because it was the will of God for Him as our Savior. Jesus had reached the point where He had been forsaken by human justice and now forsaken by His own Father. At this point, He still had all authority in heaven and on earth and could choose to ease His agony. It is here that He speaks this word and puts God and us before Himself. By His choosing and speaking this word, Jesus establishes that God's will is always best because it alone saves what is lost.

Jesus did not speak this word in a moment of delusional anguish and agony. As this word says, "Jesus, knowing that all was now finished, said (to fulfill the Scripture), 'I thirst.'" Jesus trusted and believed that the will of God is best because it is about God being and working all that is good, gracious, and right for us.

Jesus' resurrection tells the entire world that while the will of God and His ways of working it may be beyond us, it alone can always be trusted to bring us a glorious outcome. This will of God shall be done for all who believe on the Lord Jesus Christ.

Prayer "Father, . . . nevertheless, not My will, but Yours, be done."
Luke 22:42

The Suffering Word

Tuesday, Lent 5

Many yield to the illusion that all religions lead to God. This averts the potential difficulties in confessing that Christ alone is the way to God the Father. This illusion is used to prove that one is more intelligent, open minded, and compassionate. Ultimately, this illusion keeps people from putting their full faith in Christ alone as their Savior.

"I thirst" (John 19:28).

All man-made religions tell people what they can and must do to come to God and obtain His favor. The reality that Jesus Christ is the only way to the Father was born out not so much by His word of thirst, but by the response to it. With His word of thirst, the Son of God bid those there to come to Him in His lowliness and offer Him something as simple as water. And with what do they come before the Son of God? Sour vinegar.

The uniqueness of Jesus Christ is that He is God come to save us. Christ alone is God suffering our sin's unquenchable thirst and our lack of water to quench that thirst. Christ alone is God taking our sin, its thirst, and us into death so that sin and its thirst might die with Him. Christ alone is God resurrected to offer us living water. Christ alone is God coming to us, inviting one and all who thirst to come to the waters and drink "without money and without price" (Isaiah 55:1).

In the living waters of Baptism, God unites us to Christ alone, and in Him we have the only way, the only truth, and the only life that brings us to God the Father.

Prayer "Be gracious to me and hear my prayer. . . . In peace I will both lie down and sleep; for You alone, O LORD, make me dwell in safety." **Psalm 4:1, 8**

The Dying Word

Wednesday, Lent 5

For our sinful nature, the illusion that "my life is my own" is second only to its primary illusion that we are like God. Through this illusion, we seek to free ourselves from responsibility or accountability. Through this illusion, God and His Word, like truth, are expendable because neither will necessarily guarantee us what we want.

> "Father, into Your hands
> I commit My spirit!" (Luke 23:46).

Jesus knew that He was begotten of His Father and therefore belonged to the Father. As creations of God, we each belong to God. In selling ourselves to sin, mankind has rejected both God and our belonging to Him. In His own love and want for us, God sent His Son to take our flesh and shed His innocent blood to buy us back from our slavery to sin and death. Having paid the price for us with His own blood, we now belong to Jesus.

Having finished His earthly mission of saving all mankind from the slavery of sin, Jesus had one thing to do before He entered into death. With this word, Jesus returns Himself to the God and Father in whom He belonged. In giving Himself back to His Father, Jesus gives each of us who belong to Him back to His Father and ours.

In Baptism, God gives Himself to us as He unites us with Christ and we receive His eternal belonging to God. Through this divinely instituted Sacrament, we are made holy children, "who were born, not of blood nor of the will of the flesh nor of the will of man, but of God" (John 1:13). We live our birth and belonging rights through faith in Jesus Christ.

Prayer "Remember Your congregation, which You have purchased of old, which You have redeemed to be the tribe of Your heritage!" **Psalm 74:2**

The Dying Word

Thursday, Lent 5

To countless people burdened by their sins—sins of the past, big sins, or sins they struggle with and lose to daily—our sinful pride casts the illusion that "God would not want someone like me." Through this illusion, our sinful nature seeks to have a person perpetually despair of his guilt. Through this illusion, one's heart is hardened to the message of a different verdict that God alone offers to all in Jesus Christ.

> "Father, into Your hands
> I commit My spirit!" (Luke 23:46).

This word is spoken by the Son of God, who has received every type, size, and description of our sin to Himself and suffered our verdict. This word does not ignore the verdict of the Law; it simply speaks the consequent reality that this verdict has been carried out and is finished. "There is therefore now no condemnation for those who are in Christ Jesus" (Romans 8:1).

Having suffered and silenced our verdict, Jesus speaks the reality of what God wants all people to say. Through His blessed forgiveness, this word of Jesus has become our daily declaration and prayer as we live by faith in the wanting, loving, and ever-keeping hands of our God, Father, Son, and Holy Spirit.

Prayer "The LORD will fulfill His purpose for me; Your steadfast love, O LORD, endures forever. Do not forsake the work of Your hands." **Psalm 138:8**

The Dying Word

Friday, Lent 5

D o you think that eternal life is something we receive only after death? It is argued that inasmuch as eternal life is something that comes after this life, there is no purpose in letting it dominate our life in the here and now.

> "Father, into Your hands
> I commit My spirit!" (Luke 23:46).

Having come in our flesh, been crucified in our place, and then suffered hell by God forsaking Him, Jesus had let our sinful lives—past, present, and future—dominate Him on Calvary. Then Jesus spoke a word declaring the end of the domination of the here and now of sin. Jesus finished the power of all sin by suffering its eternal consequence. Death was the one last power that He would let dominate Him so that He might, three days later, dominate over it forever and for all.

Knowing that beyond death there is no opportunity for us to seek eternal life, Jesus sought it in this life by calling to His Father. Having reconciled man to God, Jesus prayed this word and brought the eternal dominion of God the Father to rule in His life here and now before death. With this prayer, Jesus brought His Father's eternal dominion of grace to all who were given to Him on the cross. When the Father reversed the here and now of death for Jesus in His resurrection, God further revealed why eternal life is for the here and now.

In Baptism, we are united with Jesus Christ, crucified and risen, and in Him, we have eternal life. Through faith in Christ, we live eternal life in the here and now for His kingdom here and there.

Prayer "Look on my affliction and deliver me. . . . Plead my cause and redeem me; give me life according to Your promise!" **Psalm 119:153–54**

The Dying Word

Saturday, Lent 5

Like heresy, sinful illusions include an element of truth in them. Death is the end of all that is sin. But it is a false illusion that our sinful nature is forever destined to die because of its sinfulness. In this way, it seeks to harden us in a quest to eat, drink, and be merry, for tomorrow we die.

> "Father, into Your hands
> I commit My spirit!" (Luke 23:46).

With this word, Jesus spoke a new reality that in Him, death is no longer an end, but a portal. Because of sin, death will always be a part of every life in this fallen world. Having received the sin of all mankind on the cross, Jesus dealt with it and emptied its power to bring death. Jesus prepared to deal with death by laying His flesh down in death as He said, "No one takes it from Me, but I lay it down of My own accord. I have authority to lay it down, and I have authority to take it up again" (John 10:18).

As He prepared to lay down His life in death, He speaks this word commending His spirit into the keeping of His Father, making death a portal to paradise and life everlasting. His bodily resurrection three days later reveals the reality that in Christ, death is no longer the end of our body or spirit.

In Baptism, we are given Christ's death so that we might have Jesus' resurrection, and a life lived by faith. "To this end Christ died and lived again, that He might be Lord both of the dead and of the living" (Romans 14:9).

Prayer "Return, O my soul, to your rest; for the LORD has dealt bountifully with you. For you have delivered my soul from death."
Psalm 116:7–8

HOLY
WEEK

The Dying Word
Palm Sunday

Bound in the illusion that we are like God, our sinful nature would have us believe that inasmuch as it will not listen to God, God surely will not listen to sinners. As closed as the sinful heart is to God, it would have us believe that God's heart is just as closed. Seeking to preserve its complete dominion over us, our sinful nature seeks by this illusion to silence any repentant prayer to God for His promised mercy.

> "Father, into Your hands
> I commit My spirit!" (Luke 23:46).

Because of our sin, we lack righteousness before God by which we may come into His presence. Having received all our sin and unrighteousness on the cross, God refused to listen to Jesus as He suffered the silence of God to His cry "Why have You forsaken Me?" Jesus suffered the deaf ear of God that each sinner deserves, in order to open the ears of God. As His word "It is finished!" meant the end of sin's power and the wrath of God, is also meant the end of God's deafness to all sinners.

Jesus prayed this word to give us the reality of a loving and listening God. With this word, Jesus not only gives Himself back to His Father, but He also gives all mankind back to God as the redeemed.

Since the first sin, God has always sought and listened to the prayers of repentant sinners. There is only one kind of person to whom God will never listen: the person who prays to Him with his own righteousness.

Only through faith in Jesus Christ and His righteousness are we made righteous and gladly received by God in person and prayer.

Prayer "Hear my prayer, O Lord; give ear to my pleas for mercy! In Your faithfulness answer me, in Your righteousness!"
Psalm 143:1

The Dying Word

Monday in Holy Week

Sinful pride's illusion is that faith is about our hanging on to God. This illusion is cast for the purpose of allowing a person to have faith, just not saving faith. In this illusion, if a person is going to have faith, that faith is in themselves and their ability to hang on to God.

> "Father, into Your hands
> I commit My spirit!" (Luke 23:46).

Bound in the power of sin, we cannot hang on to anything in this world, let alone God. Jesus is ready to enter death that He might destroy death. Note that His prayer before entering death was not "Father, I am hanging on to You so that You can receive My spirit." With this word, Jesus reveals the reality that saving faith is about believing that God hangs on to us.

God has always hung on to mankind, when we should have been let go in our sin. In His love and want to hang on to all people, God sent Christ as His hand reaching out to take hold of us in our sin, so that He could let Jesus go, to save us from our sin. Having been let go of by God, Jesus spoke this believing word and gave not only His spirit but ours also into the hands of God. Christ's bodily resurrection again proves the wisdom and saving power of such faith.

Saving faith looks only to the hand of God that it might receive His love and saving grace. Saving faith looks to Jesus Christ alone, for He held on to us and to God. In His hand alone our names have been engraved, and from His hand nothing can release or remove us.

Prayer "Into Your hand I commit my spirit; You have redeemed me, O Lord, faithful God." **Psalm 31:5**

The Dying Word

Tuesday in Holy Week

Unwilling to let us encounter the reality of our utter helplessness and need to believe in God, our sinful pride casts the illusion that we need more than God's Word for the purpose of redefining faith. Faith cannot be "the assurance of things hoped for, the conviction of things not seen" (Hebrews 11:1), because it lies beyond our abilities. By redefining faith, it becomes a conviction of things God can prove to justify believing His Word.

> "Father, into Your hands
> I commit My spirit!" (Luke 23:46).

With this word, Jesus commends His spirit into the hands of the God and Father who had just forsaken Him. Of all the words that Jesus speaks from the cross, this word seems to beg the question of why? Yes, Jesus has declared that the wrath of God was finished, but there has been no sign, no proof that God would receive Him back as His Son. So what enabled Jesus to commend His spirit into the hands of God His Father? Only the Word of God.

What did Jesus have in the midst of all His suffering and abandonment that allowed Him to believe in God His Father? One little promise found in Psalm 16: "My flesh also dwells secure. For You will not abandon my soul to Sheol, or let Your holy one see corruption" (vv. 9–10).

The wisdom of Jesus' faith was seen on that first Easter morning, when God His Father kept this promise and raised Jesus from the dead. Jesus Christ is God's Word of promise, and through this Word He creates faith in us. Through this faith, we receive a wisdom that enables us daily and hourly to commend our spirit and our lives into the hands of our ever-faithful God and heavenly Father.

Prayer "I believe; help my unbelief!" **Mark 9:24**

The Dying Word

Wednesday in Holy Week

T he people of Israel cried, "The way of the Lord is not just" (Ezekiel 33:17) because of the Lord's way of dealing with them for their hypocritical repentance (33:31). Our sinful nature seeks to raise us up as an appeals court judge to overrule the ways of the rightful Judge. This verdict reveals the success of our sinful nature to make us the judges we are not.

> "God did not send His Son into the world to condemn the world, but in order that the world might be saved through Him" (John 3:17).

Like all illusions, there is a grain of truth in this one as well. If God were just and only just, there would never have been Cain, Abel, Noah, Abraham, David, or anyone else. The first promise in the Garden of Eden was one of a just death for sin. If God were just and only just, death and eternal separation from God would have only been the result for Adam and Eve. The second promise in the Garden of Eden came after their sin; by it God revealed that He is more than just—He is also merciful and gracious.

This fulfillment of the second promise is Jesus Christ incarnate, cruci-fied, buried, and resurrected. This promise is Jesus being what we cannot be, suffering the consequence we deserve, and dying the death we cannot die to answer the demands of God's justice. The second promise is Jesus Christ resurrected in the flesh so that we who are bound in the flesh might live a new life in Him.

Living by the grace of God through faith in Jesus Christ, we live daily and hourly with God, who is more than just, and whose way is our only way to the heavenly Father.

Prayer "O LORD, be gracious to me; heal me, for I have sinned against You!" **Psalm 41:4**

The Dying Word

Maundy Thursday

In the Lord's Supper we receive the God-given gift in the God-chosen packages. Instead of the Lord's Supper being God's means of giving and working His grace in us through the body and blood of Christ, through our sinful pride it becomes our means of working ourselves in the presence of God. Satan and our sinful nature's only goal is to deny a person the blessed communion with Jesus Christ through His true body and blood given in this Holy Supper in and with and under the bread and wine.

"Do this in remembrance of Me" (Luke 22:19).

With this word, Jesus establishes that the reality of the Lord's Supper is about our receiving what He just gave. He spoke the reality of what we are to do: "Jesus took bread, and after blessing it broke it and gave it to the disciples, and said, 'Take, eat; this is My body.' And He took a cup, and when He had given thanks He gave it to them, saying, 'Drink of it, all of you, for this is My blood of the covenant, which is poured out for many for the forgiveness of sins' " (Matthew 26:26–28).

The reality of each believer's part in the Lord's Supper is to receive the bread and under this form to receive the body of Jesus Christ, and with it, all that is His. Our part is to receive the wine and under this form the blood of Jesus Christ, shed for the forgiveness of our sins.

In this blessed Sacrament, we receive again Jesus Christ and His history as we first did in our Baptism. Here Christ gives us His perfect life, suffering, sacrificial death, and resurrection, so that the work of His history in us might be strengthened and increased.

Prayer "Thanks be to God through Jesus Christ our Lord!" **Romans 7:25**

The Fulfilled Word

Good Friday

We live in a world where people, even Christians, have sinful thoughts and desires, say sinful things, and do sinful things. People get sick, suffer, and die. Limited by sin to only doing these and seeing such things, our sinful nature seeks to create doubt about the work and word of Jesus Christ on the cross.

"It is finished" (John 19:30).

With this word, Jesus reveals that He had finished drinking the cup of God's wrath, which had been poured for every sinner to drink. Having emptied this cup, He fully took the wrath of God upon Himself, and it no longer falls to us to pay the eternal penalty for our sin.

God freely offers this finish to all people. For those who believe, "there is therefore now no condemnation for those who are in Christ Jesus" (Romans 8:1). For those baptized into Christ, the eternal favor of God exists for them now. In Christ, we are given a new life and a new cup that is filled with the grace of God in the body and blood of Jesus Christ.

Living by faith in Christ and His blessed forgiveness, the baptized are not naïve about sin, suffering, death, or the grave. We simply ask, "O death, where is your victory? O death, where is your sting?" (1 Corinthians 15:55). And by faith we proclaim, "The sting of death is sin, and the power of sin is the law. But thanks be to God, who gives us the victory through our Lord Jesus Christ" (1 Corinthians 15:56–57).

Prayer "LORD, 'You are my Lord; I have no good apart from You.' For You will not abandon my soul to Sheol, or let Your holy one see corruption. You make known to me the path of life; in Your presence there is fullness of joy; at Your right hand are pleasures forevermore." **Psalm 16:2, 10–11**

The Restful Word

Holy Saturday

Limited to peddling the sounds of sin, suffering, and the silence of death, the sinful nature can only misread the silence of Christ's tomb as death's victory. Our sinful pride seeks to deny the reality of Christ's victory in death, suggesting that the silence of the tomb is the tomb's victory, so that we might doubt Christ's victory over death.

> "For God alone my soul waits in silence;
> from Him comes my salvation. . . . For
> God alone, O my soul, wait in silence, for
> my hope is from Him" (Psalm 62:1, 5).

These words of reality interpret Jesus' silence in the tomb. Having suffered through the silence of God's wrath for us and finished it, Jesus' last word on the cross was a word of faith with which He commended Himself into His Father's keeping. Jesus' silence while in the tomb speaks not of the grave's power but of His faith and confidence in His Father's power to keep and deliver Him from the grave and its power. Jesus could be silent because it was a time to let His Father, father Him.

The believer and unbeliever alike must go through many adversities. The world reads the believer's quiet silence as a surrender to those adversities. What they do not know is that for the believer, it is a time for God. Living by faith in Christ, we journey in the silence of a sure hope, allowing our heavenly Father to father us as He did His Son on to the resurrection.

Prayer "Lead me in Your truth and teach me, for You are the God of my salvation; for You I wait all the day long." **Psalm 25:5**

The Vindicated Word

Easter Sunday

There are those who deny Christ's resurrection by saying it was only spiritual. Yet, in believing this, the sinful nature separates such people from Christ's victory over all things fleshly. If Christ's victory is not over the flesh, then there is no reason for Christ and His Word to have any power over their fleshly lives. In this way, the sinful nature is free to reign and ruin at its will.

> "He is not here, for He has risen, as He said. Come, see the place where He lay. Then go quickly and tell His disciples that He has risen from the dead, and behold, He is going before you to Galilee; there you will see Him" (Matthew 28:6–7).

It may be argued that the difficulty with the Gospel's word arises from the fact that it is a complete reversal of all human reality. The real difficulty, however, arises from the fact that this word of resurrection is not a human word. This word of resurrection belongs only to Jesus Christ, because by His holy incarnation, life, crucifixion, and death, God declares Him to be the reversal of all human reality, by resurrecting Him bodily over human reality.

This "Jesus word" is spoken and offered to all because we have no such word in the reality of human bondage to sin, suffering, and death. In Baptism, God unites us to Jesus Christ, and in this union of grace, the reality of all of Jesus' words become our words of new reality in which we live by faith in Him.

Alleluia! He is risen! He is risen indeed! Alleluia!

Prayer For the joy Thine advent gave me, For Thy holy, precious Word; For Thy Baptism, which doth save me, For Thy blest Communion board; For Thy death, the bitter scorn, For Thy resurrection morn, Lord, I thank Thee and extol Thee, And in heaven I shall behold Thee. (*TLH* 207:6)

Notes
Ash Wednesday and the Days Following

Notes

Lent: Week One

Notes
Lent: Week Two

Notes

Lent: Week Three

Notes
Lent: Week Four

Notes
Lent: Week Five

Notes
Holy Week